Burningword
Ninety-Nine

A SELECTED ANTHOLOGY OF POETRY

2001-2011

EDITED BY
ERIK AUSTIN DEERLY

© 2012 by Burningword & the authors

All rights reserved. Published in the United States by Burrdowning Press, Carmel IN.

Burningword Literary Journal (ISSN 2161-8992 print / ISSN 2157-7366 online) is a quarterly publication focusing on emerging writers of poetry and short fiction. This book is a selected anthology of poetry submitted to and published by the journal between 2001 and 2011. All poems herein may also be found online at burningword.com.

Owing to space limitations, notes and acknowledgments begin on page 161.

Publishing Editor & Creative Director
Erik Austin Deerly

Editor In Chief
Anita M. Garza

Intern
Alisha Referda

Burrdowning Press
PO Box 217
Carmel IN 46062 USA

ISBN 978-0-9857888-0-3

Contents

Erik Austin Deerly — 1
INTRODUCTION

Doug Tanoury — 3
THE GHOST OF MADAME CÉZANNE | 001

Doug Tanoury — 4
BAD WEATHER | 002

Doug Tanoury — 5
SPARROWS | 003

John Sweet — 6
THE FIRST BODY OF THE SEASON | 004

Chad Rood — 8
SMOKED...COOKED | 005

Chad Rood — 9
SONNET INKLING | 006

John Sweet — 10
THIS IS THE SOUND OF CROWS | 007

John Sweet — 12
ONE | 008

Anita Garza — 14
FIVE HAIKUS | 009

Michael William Giberson — 15
SURVIVOR | 010

John Sweet — 16
SWIMMING THROUGH THE BLOOD OF HISTORY | 011

Michael Carano <small>NEITHER HERE NOR THERE | 012</small>	**19**
Michael Carano <small>THE HIGHLAND THEATER LOBBY AT THE AIDS FUND-RAISER | 013</small>	**21**
Kelley Jean White <small>FARMALL | 014</small>	**22**
Kelley Jean White <small>FISH PERFUME | 015</small>	**23**
Bill Wunder <small>VIETNAM REVISITED | 016</small>	**24**
Bill Wunder <small>EARTH MOTHER | 017</small>	**25**
Bill Wunder <small>WHISPERS FROM GOD | 018</small>	**27**
Bill Wunder <small>TEARS OF AFRICA | 019</small>	**28**
Michael Crowley <small>I ONCE KNEW A WOMAN | 020</small>	**29**
Michael Crowley <small>THE LORD SAID | 021</small>	**31**
Richard Jordan <small>THERAPY AND DREAMS | 022</small>	**32**
Richard Jordan <small>THE POET INSPECTS PRECISION ENGINEERING | 023</small>	**35**

Richard Jordan
WHATEVER HAPPENED? | 024 — 37

Richard Jordan
A POEM WRITTEN AFTER AN EVENING OF READING
DARWIN AND THE SCRIPTURES, IN THAT ORDER | 025 — 38

John Sweet
THE POET TAKES HIS PLACE IN THE ACTUAL WORLD | 026 — 39

Bill Wunder
EXILE IN ROOM 101 | 027 — 41

Bill Wunder
PHU CAT, VIETNAM—1970 | 028 — 42

Bill Wunder
RELIGION | 029 — 43

John Sweet
IN THE EMPTY HOUSE
WHERE NO ONE BELIEVES IN EMPTY HOUSES | 030 — 44

John Sweet
DEFINING MYSELF UNCLEARLY IN THE SEASON OF CROWS | 031 — 46

Christina Croft
COLLISION OF MADNESS AND SIN | 032 — 48

Christina Croft
BLINDED TWILIGHT | 033 — 49

Christina Croft
AGITATED ANGST | 034 — 50

Yun Wei
RUNNING RED | 035 — 51

Yun Wei
THE PLAYGROUND AFTER RAIN | 036 — 54

Yun Wei
TO SOMEONE SITTING ON THE BLUE-GLASS ROOF | 037 — 57

Sam Vaknin
CUTTING TO EXISTENCE | 038 — 58

Harley Hill
TONGUE TIED | 039 — 59

Harley Hill
RAT TAILED WANTING | 040 — 60

John Sweet
WEIGHING THE WORD LOVE ON BROKEN SCALES | 041 — 61

Christopher Swan
SUNSHINE STATE | 042 — 63

Christopher Swan
EARLY LIGHT | 043 — 65

Christopher Swan
RIVER RUN | 044 — 66

Kelley Jean White
WHAT DO YOU EAT WHEN YOU'RE NOT IN LOVE? | 045 — 67

Kelley Jean White
BRITTLE | 046 — 68

Carol Parris Krauss
LUNCH @ LA BELLE | 047 — 70

John Sweet
PROVING DALI'S EXISTENCE WITH
WORDS AND THE SPACES BETWEEN THEM | 048

72

Bill Wunder
MEMORIAL DAY 2002 | 049

74

Janet Buck
THIS OLD CHAIR | 050

76

Janet Buck
SO THIS HOW AGAPE READS | 051

78

Janet Buck
SHARP ICE | 052

80

Janet Buck
RUG BURN | 053

82

Janet Buck
THE WASTELAND WHERE YOUR BODY SLEPT | 054

84

Janet Buck
GRAMMY'S TOOLS | 055

86

Patrick Seth Williams
UNDERNEATH | 056

88

Patrick Seth Williams
GINSBERG AT BREAKFAST | 057

89

Patrick Seth Williams
VOODOO MANIFESTATIONS | 058

90

Christine Hamm
HYSTERICAL BLINDNESS | 059

92

John Sweet — 94
AMONG THE DEAD AND DYING | 060

Janet Buck — 96
YOLKI BLUES | 061

John Sweet — 98
VAN GOGH TAKES UP PAINTING AGAIN, 122 YEARS AFTER HIS SUICIDE | 062

Janet Buck — 100
ALLERGIES TO IVORY | 063

Janet Buck — 102
ASSUMPTION | 064

Keith Webb — 104
SO MUCH LESS THAN SENSUAL | 065

M. R. Benning — 106
CURLED AND JARRED | 066

M. R. Benning — 107
THE BIOLOGY OF JIMMY SMITH | 067

Janet Buck — 109
INSIDE A NAME | 068

Janet Buck — 111
SUDDENLY IT'S SOLITAIRE | 069

John Sweet — 113
PHOTOGRAPHING THE CIVIL WAR | 070

Janet Buck — 115
A SPEECH BEFORE THE SPLATTERED BLOOD | 071

Robert Bohm — MOUNTAINS | 072 — 117

Robert Bohm — SACRED | 073 — 119

Barclay Kenyon — FIREGARDEN (TRIPTYCH 3) | 074 — 121

Arlene Ang — THEY SAY | 075 — 125

Arlene Ang — FINAL DRAW | 076 — 126

Duane Locke — SOLITUDE OR ISOLATION | 077 — 128

Duane Locke — LET ME BE SO | 078 — 130

Rebecca Jung — POEM BEFORE A WAR | 079 — 131

Rebecca Jung — THE COLLARBONE | 080 — 132

Janet Buck — THE POOLSIDE CHAT | 081 — 133

Kelley Jean White — BRICKHOUSE BLUES | 082 — 135

Joseph Armstead — ANGEL AMONGST ASHES | 083 — 137

Janet Buck — 140
MUSTARD SEEDS | 084

Rhonda Ward — 141
MISSING LIMBS | 085

Rhonda Ward — 142
BETWEEN SCHOOL AND HOME | 086

Rhonda Ward — 143
PORTRAIT OF THE PORCH IN SUMMER | 087

Rhonda Ward — 144
GRAY MATTER | 088

Janet Buck — 145
A ROSE TO PRESS | 089

c. e. laine — 146
WHY I WROTE MY FIRST LIVING WILL | 090

John Sweet — 147
A SMALL DOG, BLEEDING | 091

John Sweet — 149
FIRST PORTRAIT OF MARIA, IN THE STYLE OF DALI | 092

Michael Lee Johnson — 151
DOVE POEM | 093

Erik Austin Deerly — 152
KENT | 094

Erik Austin Deerly — 154
DEAR HARVEY | 095

Madeleine J. Deerly — 155
SOME THINGS I HAVE LEARNED THAT
I WOULD BE MUCH BETTER OFF NOT KNOWING | 096

JE Baker — 156
TRAIL | 097

Ivor Irwin — 158
MARRIAGE | 098

Ivor Irwin — 159
6 A.M.- 9 A.M. | 099

Notes On The Contributors — 161

Erik Austin Deerly

INTRODUCTION

Burningword Literary Journal was founded in June 2000 as an Internet-only publication (www.burningword.com). It's not that we hated paper, but rather we couldn't afford it. We chose to use the tools we had on hand and we planned to add the print version after a year or so. We launched issue 01 of our *all-digital* endeavor on January 01, 2001 at 01:01:01 Greenwich Mean Time—or *010101010101*.

Ten years later, after a few changes in direction and 58 issues of consistently fantastic submissions, we finally got around to the print version we had promised. This anthology contains some of our favorite poems from those dark ages, before print. *Burningword* has always focused on emerging writers. The poets in this anthology each contributed their time, encouragement, and talent—generously—far beyond simply sending in submissions. I offer them each a huge thanks.

The book is assembled in chronological order, for the most part. Feel free to read it as a timeline or to just dig in anywhere. And please, work your way to the "Notes On The Contributors" section, where you can find out a bit more about the poets.

Doug Tanoury

THE GHOST OF MADAME CÉZANNE | 001

Madame Cézanne
Haunts my study
In ghostlike apparition
She appears
Again and again
With cheeks painted a bit too red
And makeup caked across her face

Each time I see her
I think she wears
The countenance of strife
The shades of sadness
She never speaks but
Sits silently in a chair
Posed in resentment

Her eyes angry openings
Her mouth closed and pouting
Her jaw clenched
A face hard
And humorless
She is a model of domestic troubles
Wearing a green hat

Doug Tanoury

BAD WEATHER | **002**

Whenever I saw him
I felt the cold
A kind of deep chill
That passed through me
Numbing my insides
And the ice that formed
On the outer edges of my words
Was skin tingling
In the same way
His kisses were snowflakes
Melting on my cheeks

I would always wish him gone
Just as I would hope
For winter's passing
And long for a trace of color
In the pencil sketch landscape
That is February
And now that he is
A season past
There is mildness in the air
And a stirring in the earth
Of things ready to grow

Doug Tanoury

SPARROWS | 003

Sparrows perch on a narrow ledge
Half hidden in the eaves
Of my awning and from the window
I can watch them mating
A hop and a flutter of wings
Another hop and more flutter
And in the smallness of their love
They resemble shot glasses
Stacked two high
One within another

The sparrows have built three nests
Half hidden in shadows of my awning
Each one a weave of honey blonde grass
Into a unkempt mass
That is oddly symmetrical
Like the disheveled hair of three girls
Sitting side-by-side on a bench by the lake
Each one tangled and mussed
In the very same direction
On an afternoon in March

John Sweet

THE FIRST BODY OF THE SEASON | 004

a year since
the god of
starving dogs

the person i was
left behind like
so much
shed skin

the person i am
content to sit by
this second story
window
at twilight

willing to believe
the ovens will
never be fired up
again

and next door
a baby cries
or maybe a mother

and two days ago
the first body
of the season
was pulled from t
he river and
named

a small moment
buried beneath
centuries of
brutality but it
stays with me

whatever can't be
forgotten
worried to death
instead

Chad Rood

SMOKED...COOKED | **005**

thick bones and hanging skin
are pinned under six wool blankets.

white skull covered in red wet skin
soaks in soggy pillow.

oven iron holds oak fire
as an alto woman's lounge smoked song cracks through a single speaker

a cigarrette burns
and sleeps moist
in a coffee can of butts,
buried,
smoldering in the swelter,
smoking like the steam
off a pot of simmering water.

a breath weezes
and a throat gargles.

watery blue eyes
slip out from under
greasy lids,

they wiggle
then freeze
then fail to see.

Chad Rood

SONNET INKLING | 006

exchange a plastic bag full of your blood
for sticky mint green paper.
exchange sticky mint green paper
for caviar like fake pearls covered in wet ink
inside one rusty chain link.

exchange sticky mint green paper for
pasture covered in dead angus,
holstein and jersey cattle.

exchange sticky mint green paper
for a silver spiral binding,
colored fluid and wood shavings,
and a lamp to tickle them.

ink black light
with linked white shavings.

John Sweet

THIS IS THE SOUND OF CROWS | 007

and she is there
at the edge of the field

she is gathering flowers
and the sky
surrounds her

we are not lost

we are not forgotten

we are hopeful
and the book of days is empty
and in the town we left behind
the poets have all
been hung

this is the truth
everywhere

this is the sound of crows
after three months with
no rain and she
is there

she is gathering flowers
and they turn to dust in her
delicate hands and
the poem inside her heart was
never meant to be read

was never
meant to be written
and the dust falls through
her fingers with the slow
grace of angels

and we are far from home
but hopeful

John Sweet
ONE | 008

the poem is
just beneath the
skin

the skin is pale and
easily opened

what happens though
is this

i find myself
out of words

out of breath on
the front steps with
the roses i bought
already fading

with apologies falling
dead
from my lips

and if i'm not a
person you could ever
love and if
you don't have the strength
to hate me
then what?

we are all afraid in
the thin air
of passing days

held to the ground by
the sheer grey enormity
of the sky

by the lack of
possibility

one among us just
waiting for the
perfect moment to step
forward and be
crucified

Anita Garza

FIVE HAIKUS | **009**

Tossing and turning
Awake, I am, in the night
Slumber will not come

Safely protected
In your arms, I want to be
From all things evil

Daylight brings laughter
In the heart of the city
Night, dangers abound

Children dream pleasures
Joyful and playful their lives
Pray, they find their way

Spring rain sparkles bright
Winter, dormant life awaits
Spring rain makes life new

Michael William Giberson

SURVIVOR | 010

Should the dead rise
To take your stead,

And you lay
Bleeding in his place,

The silent covenant
Between you bred

Of circumstance
Would not alter.

Do not rage your dissolving heart.
Do not rail God's dusty plan.

John Sweet

SWIMMING THROUGH THE BLOOD OF HISTORY | 011

and i am tired of reading
all of these words i wrote as if
i thought i might actually
know something

i am tired
of these empty notebooks
like mute accusations

if you were in this room
right now
you would smell desperation

would feel a small cool breeze as
the storm pushes its way north

picture it

three years in this house
and i know none of my neighbors

ten years in this town
and i refuse to call it home

and did i pray
at my father's bedside
in the last days before his death?

no

and does this
make me a bad person?

i've been told that it does

and there is a man
who returns what i send him with
a note that says
"these are not poems"
and there is the possibility that
he's right

there are my hands
crippled with self-doubt

burned and then healed
and then burned again until
they refuse to acknowledge the
simple pain of passing days

and if i don't call myself
an artist
then i can't be crucified
as a witch

the logic is subtle
but it's there

think of war

Michael Carano

NEITHER HERE NOR THERE | **012**

Otis, in all his mercy, on some lost tablet,
etched for granite minds his stony commandments:
Elevator decorum demands agreement,
look forward, keep space within a space,
appendages shall never rise in gesture,
nor brush the flanks of erected riders,
and weathered souls?–the topic weather!
the irony of the getting off before got on.

And, so too, in a dusty corner of Metro's chamber,
locked in a file without a key,
the rules of disengagement have a proper seal,
codified and passed by council,
(forgotten but by one forgotten civil servant)
for rider's (with riders), the commuting clan.
Have proper change, expression changeless,
avert the gaze, less it acknowledge
the trip has no sure destination,
and always be an unspectacular specter
traveling in a tram stuffed with empty ghosts.

Oh, we've seen them before, while awaiting the call
at the dentist office, leafing National Geographic
of an unpeopled place, those imposing, inscrutable faces,
the blank eyed and stony forms, gray seaward facing,
expressionless, looking like wayward bicuspids

incisively needing bridgework to bring there to here:
those distant looks embracing distance
in the silence of an ethereal, blank stare.

But who among us does not wait
For one to twist upon his base and
falling to the ground with a heavy thud,
blink awake the heavy lids upon its face,
unsmack his frozen, muted lips,
unstick the ears and take in sea-sound,
and roll downhill upon the ground,
laughing and squealing with delightful spree,
plunge splashing into the unknown ocean.

Michael Carano

THE HIGHLAND THEATER LOBBY AT THE AIDS FUND-RAISER

See her, over there,
it's Solo Sandy,
The girl with a one-eyed Siamese cat
(Half-Mongolian, I've been told),
smoking a cig during intermission
at a "Surprisingly Sassy" show.
Standing in the theater lobby,
black hair and gown, dark eyes,
Mediterranean complexion, she
looks alone like a kidnapped Helen,
amidst soft and feathered barbarians
each extravagantly trying to outdo
the simple, classic elegance
of this quiet beauty, this
stranger in a strange land.
She, unaware of the corpse-littered battlefield,
never notices the vanquished,
the slain victims of her bloodless victory,
nor the suitor preparing the ship.

Kelley Jean White

FARMALL | 014

I am pleased to have Arthur sit
on my lawn for the Old Home Day parade.
He and Millie were good friends to my parents.
I know he and Peter feel quite alone
now that she is gone.
I know it has been a difficult year for Peter,
what with the surgery on his hips and the brief
failed marriage, but they have the church people
to help and they know everyone.
Arthur is one of the last people to have cows in town.
I love to see the tin roof on his barn reflect
the sunset off the mountain. Jenny did a good job too.
She got two pictures of Peter driving the tractor.
One close up where he looks strong and wiry,
not at all sickly or limited, and one where
he waves, and his hand is the hand of a leader,
announcing the ripe corn and haystacks
on the flatbed truck float.
The tractor itself looks magnificent. Funny
I didn't notice it in the parade. The flag waving
in front of the high grill, the majestic wheels.
It's been months now since August.
I could just mail the pictures up,
but I think I'll wait and take them by at Christmas,
bring my mother and the children.
It's right on the way to the good Christmas tree fields.
I'd be nice to see the animals in the snow.

Kelley Jean White

FISH PERFUME | **015**

trout new out of the water smell
power and cold and heavy moss dark
I have put two drops from the bottle
behind my ears, white shoulders, quiet
true my hands trailing the nets gravid
with dying and dulling eye stare
I want this boy to remember me in
dusk light when we row our fathers'
boat home pale before the rising moon

Bill Wunder

VIETNAM REVISITED | 016

Distant thunder rides Asian wind,
rumbles across oceans,
echoes down years.
Who sent this awful noise of war?
Deafening roar of pain, of death,
made whores of village girls,
made us climb, veins on fire,
a stairway to smack heaven.
Can I buy you for this pack of cigarettes?
Unmoved by crying almond eyes.
Burning mountain, ignite the sky
with death's hot desire.
Acrid napalm smoke billows
higher, higher,
over a raped country's dying sigh.
Alien, tortured forms
locked in final embrace,
shining wet in monsoon rain,
washed clean of blood.
What will cleanse us
of our guilt and shame?

Bill Wunder

EARTH MOTHER | 017

Tinged silver-blue

by moonbeams,
luminous earth mother
hums with ethereal music.
Her velvet footsteps
pass the spiked fence
of coastal cedars,
solitary sentinels
old as time,
guard the night.

Luna moths,
iridescent ghosts
in magic moonlight
float among fireflies,
a starscape on earth,
fallen on a sleepy meadow.

Mother goddess,
fertile nymph-spirit rests,
bedded down on pillow moss
deliciously fragrant
while angel-fingered fronds
caress her face.
Cicada serenade,

a moondust lullaby
of echoed dreams
envelopes her.
She sighs, sleeping
among ferns, at peace.

Bill Wunder

WHISPERS FROM GOD | **018**

On my knees,
our familiar rendezvous,
waiting for you
as I always do,
to speak in whispers
only my heart may hear.

Silence.
I know you are here,
your presence is wind
caressing my upturned face.
I await forgiveness,
offering neither reason
nor explanation.
I await boundless joy,
lifting me beyond
a sea of transgression.

I am overwhelmed
by the quiet,
cold abandonment
of a fall from grace.

Bill Wunder

TEARS OF AFRICA | **019**

No neon glare
on the plains of Africa,
no streetlights
in the Serengeti,
only night,
black as espresso.
Parched earth revived
by generations of tears;
Lazarus land.
Hopelessness
of hunger closes in like hyenas.
Dream of them.

Dawn renews despair,
a second language here.
Red dust swirls
its death dance
with seeds of faith,
mere wishes upon the wind.
Children dressed only
in distended bellies,
adorned with flies.
I do not look them in the eye.

Michael Crowley

I ONCE KNEW A WOMAN | **020**

I once knew a woman as sharp
as a spike, (or is it a tack?)
and as hard as nails,
who thought she could fly
and blazed like a meteor
—no that's not right—
sparkled like those sparklers
that are so hard to light.
I studied her body,
would read it like a book.
She had moveable parts and
parts that stood still
as the wind in the trees
with places to kiss
and down on her arms.
And this was a time when
women had hair and were sharp
as a tack or that razor blade
you always played with
and always got cut
and the blood would be much
darker than the red you imagine.

I remember liking that woman
like the force of the tide.
We would walk around

in the city at night
or go for a ride and you
could smoke then and it was
great to walk and smoke and make words,
blow rings at the neon lights.
I once knew a woman
a shout in the street,
or a sound that makes you
suddenly turn and check
over your shoulder
for what ever might be there,
but never is,
but you're left with a little
unnamable fear.
I once knew a woman like that.

Michael Crowley

THE LORD SAID | 021

It was easier before
there were so many of them.
You could keep tabs,
help out a Roman or Greek,
check in with the Chosen.
They'd slice up their sheep,
roll some rocks around
and scream at the sky.
I'd give them green pastures and sleep.

But now it's totally out of control.
Who can keep up?
I mean there's what's left
of the birds of the air
and lilies of the field
to consider.
And if I turn my back
to intervene in Andromeda,
they set out to slaughter
one another
and send me the souls
of their children
as if I had room in my heart
or any tears left.

Richard Jordan

THERAPY AND DREAMS | **022**

I pay a therapist $90 an hour
to say Aaawww... Which is what
I want to hear. And she's awfully
cute with her little pout and pucker.
So, you see, it's entirely symbiotic.
The problem with me, she surmises,
is that I'm afraid to get in touch
with my inner child.
She may have something there.

For I have this recurring dream
of a beautiful blonde vixen in pigtails,
hiding Turkish Taffy under a Mickey Mouse
tank top. It's always hot and humid in my dreams,
so gooey globs stick to her nipples
as she pulls out the candy
and offers me a bite or two.
But its only a dream!, I yell,
as I run frantically for cover
in the nearby bushes,
being but a young boy,
lacking pubic hair,
and frightened of cavities.

In the bushes, I am greeted
by a giant hedgehog, who licks
and licks the clothes
clear from my body, except for my socks,
which are not very tasty, apparently.
And just when I'm getting accustomed
to saliva and spines, the feisty critter
turns into God and fries
the taffy temptress with
a crooked bolt of lightning.
Then he turns to me and proclaims
with booming voice (because he's God):
My son, where I come from,
$90 an hour is rather steep.
I know a lovely lady
who can set you straight
in three easy installments
of a mere $19.99,
but you must act fast.
At that, he vanishes with a poof,
leaving behind, as proof of his existence,
a stack of glossy business cards
 and a few gray whiskers.

For some reason, that's the point
at which I invariably wake up
and check my pulse, which
is the pulse of a middle-aged man
with a wife who lives 500 miles away,
two mortgages, a boss with perpetual
sardine breath, a cat who misses
the litter box, and a therapist
who's writing a Masters Thesis
on dreams and hallucinosis.

Richard Jordan

THE POET INSPECTS PRECISION ENGINEERING | 023

It was a lovely morning.
The birds outside were chipper,
my bowels were fine, and I was
about to do something very important,
or at least somewhat creative, until
I unscrewed my precision engineered
mechanical pencil to inspect the ultrafine
graphite and the crafty
Japanese workmanship.

Engineers are so darn fastidious.
Their toaster ovens are shiny
and crumbless. Their microwaves glisten
inside and out. They sweep
the sinewy brown strands
and toe jam from the space between
the foot of the bed
and the polished antique chest,
which is packed optimally with potpourri.
flannel nighties, and a spare set
of metric Allen wrenches.

I, by contrast, do my best
to avoid mysterious, dark crevices.
At night, I wrap my arms tightly
around my wife's waist to keep

from falling off the end
of the bed into the creepiness.
When my wife is away, I sleep
on the decaying couch in my study,
and imagine that the old, creaking
mechanisms are happy crickets
procreating under a winking moon.

I also eat fat bacon and fried eggs
on buttered rolls, chain-smoke
unfiltered Camels, and laze
in front of the TV all day watching
re-runs of 70's sitcoms and telethons.
But all that is another story.

Note to myself:
Buy a fountain pen.

Richard Jordan

WHATEVER HAPPENED? | 024

Whatever happened to that crazy old bugger?
You know, the guy who wore a filthy wool
cap all summer long? He had torn, greasy trousers,
and his shirt was held together with safety pins.

One time, I gave him a few cigarettes,
three, I think, and he patted me on the butt
and whispered in my ear, somewhat accusingly,
"Rasputin only eats raw lamb,
and sometimes boiled carrots".

Last time I saw him, he was fishing
for bicycle tires in the Potomac River.
I was jogging by, and he adjusted his crotch in my general direction
while giving me the one finger salute.

I suppose now that it's cold,
he's living in a shelter downtown,
passing out soap and handkerchiefs
to all the bag ladies who stop by for biscuits,
gravy, and some good, old-fashioned groping.

Every now and then, he stares out
a cracked, dirty window on the third floor
and snorts at the pathetic gnome-like creatures
on the sidewalk below,
randomly bumping into one another
on the way to Hell.

Richard Jordan

A POEM WRITTEN AFTER AN EVENING OF READING DARWIN AND THE SCRIPTURES, IN THAT ORDER

The master magician waved his wand,
And I tumbled from a long, black sleeve,
An ornery five-legged dragon, coughing
Up flames and charred feathers. With a sneeze,
He turned me into a rabid rodent,
Sending his accomplice into a panic,
As she lifted her skirt, and danced a jig
Across the stage. Next, he snapped
His fingers, transforming me into a troll,
Complete with oily facial blemishes
And patches of dark fur in mysterious,
Yet sensible places. And this is how
I shall remain, having sawed my creator
In two, after poking him with a blunt,
Shiny sword, whilst devouring his
bony, but delicious assistant.
But there's no reason for alarm.
They didn't feel a thing.
And the only blood spilled
Was my own.

John Sweet

THE POET TAKES HIS PLACE IN THE ACTUAL WORLD

fuck this idea of
poetry reaching back to
embrace the past

i will not worship
the martyred or the immortal

it's enough to be stuck in
this town of defeated old men
as they shuffle aimlessly
up and down anonymous streets

it's enough to watch the
factories burn

and i have driven in every direction
and i have seen nothing but
more of the same
and i am only waiting for the news
that reagan is dead

i am only waiting to hear
from a friend
who hasn't written in a decade
that all is forgiven

and i have a job that will never be
anything worth describing
and i have a son who will someday
want nothing more than to
escape his father

what i give you hear is a
pale blue november sky bleached to white at the edges

the drone of a plane and the
sound of wind through bare trees
and there is a house of
delicate bones in this picture
that i call my home

there is a river that holds
the body of
a fifteen year-old boy

it doesn't bother me that i've
outlived him
but maybe it should

Bill Wunder

EXILE IN ROOM 101 | 027

Life has had its way with me.
I am exiled,
to a chair in this hotel room,
counting lines in wallpaper.
Lines so straight, sharp
you could shave with them.
Imprisoned with me;
vertical cellmates.

My life revolves around me,
gliding along walls.
Resignation
brings retreat,
refuge,
in the written word.
I rise above,
free from form,
look down quiet,
velvet halls
leading to a lobby
full of strangers,
checking out,
resuming lives
I have not lived.

Bill Wunder

PHU CAT, VIETNAM—1970 | 028

Explosions varumpf
across red clay valley,
tongue-fucking my ears.
Micro jet loops,
carves new hole
in earth's shoulders.
Sound delayed by distance,
sight not far enough.
Monsoon rains death,
but cannot cleanse.
Addictions birthed here,
reunions in hell gather here.
Heroin high,
never been lower.
Mama san knows,
gums betel nut;
red mouth, no teeth.
Smirking,
we will all go,
one way or another.
I fly away, never leave.

Bill Wunder

RELIGION | 029

Breathe me.
Part your lips,
draw me in
deeply.
Hunger for me,
want me,
I am all
you require.

Taste me.
Lick my salt,
I lie thick
on your tongue,
like ash spewed
from a volcano.
Feel my tremors,
thirst for me
in the desert.
I am like rain,
I will wash
you clean.

See me,
watch me
love you.
Close your eyes,
feel me enter
the temple.
Love is religion.

John Sweet

**IN THE EMPTY HOUSE
WHERE NO ONE BELIEVES IN EMPTY HOUSES**

in the empty house
where no one believes in
empty houses
truth is not an object
with any value

a man says *i love you*
to his wife
or he doesn't
and either way she has
already left him

a child is found murdered
in the bathroom and
then another
and then three more

the words
there is something wrong here
are left unspoken

the refrigerator hums
and the clocks run backwards
and the kitten is two months old
but will have to be
given away

and why should it live in the face of these
five drowned children?

the answer depends on who you ask
and it's too fucking hot today
for these abstractions

say the word five times
and get it over with

dead dead
dead dead dead

go to the kitchen to find
a cold beer

call your wife's name and wait
the rest of your life
for an answer

John Sweet

DEFINING MYSELF UNCLEARLY IN THE SEASON OF CROWS | 031

standing in the
yellow light of december
trying to believe in war

casting a shadow along the edge
of whiskey hill road

i am not a ghost yet but have
been playing with
the idea of disappearing

have been considering that
what i may actually be afraid of
is happiness

that what i may actually be
in love with is fear

i spent twenty-seven years fighting
not to be my father's son
then married a woman who wanted
only those things i was
unwilling to give

found myself in a falling house
with the need to
inflict my anger upon others

and it's not that
i'm opposed to vengeance
and it's not that i don't believe
in freedom

it's that i have walked through
the screaming crowds promoting
their own self-righteous hatred outside of abortion clinics
and i have no faith in their god

i have no use for their dogma

i will not be branded a witch
by anyone as lost
as myself

Christina Croft

COLLISION OF MADNESS AND SIN | **032**

stealth mode activated
shiny, jagged memories escape; soar
scorched blasts of my reused, mental sponge
feast upon an uneven, blood red core
which seeps with mutilated slivers
of misplaced truths, wretched acts
Sh! I dare not speak, nor even think
decomposed dreams of wailing; torment
haunt my midnight spirit; twist into a merciless rage
hindsight bites with icy fangs that slowly drip
with no one to accuse, except my unspoken name
scent of an aged soul smoldering cries out
weeps of regret forge from within
my victims now will sense my collapse
a soldier no more; not even a man
alas, I'm exiled to radically rule
dominion in my death land

Christina Croft

BLINDED TWILIGHT | 033

Red hot, smashed phrases, spread
to burn her pale, scarred wishes
of soft, blue, cotton candy yesterdays.
Twirls of slush ridden, rotten promises
now engulf her exhausted spirit; attack her need
to feed and breathe of earthbound magic.
She craves to toss his maddening,
anger kissed words aside; drink
in soothing relief; full tide of calm slumber.
Nightscape whispers quietly laugh,
tell her to dance, join the living;
escape his soured, dark vision,
that bruises everything, anything.
Bolt of sharpened, jagged reality jolts
her to cough up some nerve and stand.
Future twilights shall not blink quickly
to be blinded from her sorrow;
she knows one life, one soul
are trapped only in this mystical flash.
Without hesitation she packs,
leaving wasted words, mind blowing fits,
and lies to slowly drown in her aftermath.

Christina Croft

AGITATED ANGST | 034

Cooled, brittle magma
angrily tastes defeat; cracks.
Full moon stains
of red wine relaxed; spilt.
I peer through blackened holes,
perpetual pits
that singe my sub-zero,
yellowed bones with contempt.
Yet, you live to breathe
of glorious human tales
and lick of their mortal,
delicious, fearful wails.
I aged, rotted
in your midnight hurricanes,
no sleep; hunger buried, saturated
by your seamless terror.
I shall not weep,
nor attain you for your sins.
Feel my bottomless rage; gasp
as it begins to frantically boil,
escape, then seep
into your poisonous brew
of unjust eternal afterglow.

Yun Wei

RUNNING RED | 035

Blood doesn't drip,
It runs
Like a river of fugitives.

A blanket is music notes,
Warmed and feathered
Until an eight-year old cheek
Can sing its softness
My cheek
As my mother's lips poured a story
The story of my great-grandmother
In the Cultural Revolution
The officials had raided the house
But it wasn't enough
So they took needles of sleek bamboo
And pricked her fingers
One by one
It was a common use of torture in those days
Effective
They found the secret stash of opium and jewels

My mother's lips had become soundless
But I could see the words roll on the blanket

I squeezed my eyes closed
Lashes embedded in skin

And tried to imagine what it
Would feel like, having my fingers pricked
One by one
All I can see are the splinters on the needles
Then flesh sagging under grief
A fear that crawls and scratches
From the heart
Peeking through the ribs
It spreads like a virus
Higher, colder
I want to swallow it before it shows its face

Skin rips.

Blood doesn't drip
It runs
Like a river of fugitives
In a slow trickle down my arms
It makes roads, streets, and avenues
Each running to a different place
The patterns look so bright
Red lantern of marriage
Binding of a book
Wide mouth of a clown
They all laugh at me
Sleek bamboo eyes

Laugh at me
Laugh at my red fingers
Laugh at my soundless lips
Laugh at the people who will never
Touch my hands again

Except, maybe
My great-granddaughter

Yun Wei

THE PLAYGROUND AFTER RAIN | **036**

Slash across the skin. Black.
As an accidental murder of ink;
Dropped pen stabbing into sand
The playground after rain,
Where the only thing that could move
Stiff, wet air is the sound of a swing,
Its chains dipped in rust
Screams drip down and through metallic prison circles
Screams of Peace being raped
Slash, slash, slash the skin.

I swing higher to dizziness,
past rushing pictures of spray-painted green
Because I do not want to see.

This moment.
A room filled with the thick breathing of anger I can
Feel crawling up my leg 5,000 miles away
I smell the impatient smoke
Circling above these men's heads
The oil they sweat, the blood they use for sautéed fish in
Holiness
"Terrorist bombing at the World Trade Center and the Pentagon today."

I lose my glasses into the gray mass above
Because I do not want to see.

This second.
Small brown eyes so easily punctured with a knife
Cotton-candy flesh so perfectly carved into pieces
To drench a navy-and-white uniform
Waterfall, black pigtails devoured by the thick
Eyebrows of a brain swimming in storms.
"In Japan, eight elementary students slain by mentally unbalanced man."

I hang my head back to let my hair suffocate in the sand
Because I do not want to see.

This breath.
Last of many last ones shakes, singing in front of a fan
A paper cut infected into scabs of hate sawed at songs of
Mother and son, father and son, sister and brother?
Mouths gaped open spit, glaze the streets of disbelief,
Paint fists with red frustration, protest the death of gods.
"Nepal's royal family was massacred by Crown Prince Dipendra, who then committed suicide."

I watch tears blur inky words down the newspaper.
Frozen faces turned gray at the point
where two walls and a ceiling meet.
Because I do not want to see.

Tears washed over the punctured corpse of Peace.

It lies in the corner.

Insect remains on windowsills.

Hemorrhage. Truth. Beauty. Love. Freedom. Bleed.

Human eyes see, human throats swallow silence by the spoonful.

Swinging, I swallow wind and try to think in the middle of spray-painted Death.

Green.

Yun Wei

TO SOMEONE SITTING ON THE BLUE-GLASS ROOF | 037

Your fingers plucked hairy screams out of the window
Running along the wooden frame of a picture
Where sun melted skin with a smile

Black was air and air was black.

Glass dripping, crying to the places that blood could not reach
Every particle of contradiction, strength,
Courage under your hair follicles are
Pillars that hold the roof up over
My well-waxed baldness.

You jumped over lines of black
Barely touching the ink with your toes
Hurdled across the pages until
A fiber snapped and ripped.

Melted dreams that made a puddle at my feet were
Gathered into a bowl and painted on the roof
The blue of a sky that birds would give their wings for
The glass of a million ethereal words
Waiting
Like the final notes of Moonlight Sonata…

Sam Vaknin

CUTTING TO EXISTENCE | **038**

My little brother cuts himself into existence.
With razor tongue I try to shave his pain,
he wouldn't listen.
His ears are woolen screams, the wrath
of heartbeats breaking to the surface.
His own Red Art.
When he cups his bleeding hands
the sea of our childhood
wells in my eyes
wells in his veins
like common salt.

Harley Hill

TONGUE TIED | 039

I don't know how to say things anymore,
Whether what I say is any good,
Or merely crap that has collected
At the mouth of the pipe
All those years since shutdown,
All those years ago, blasting outwards,
Yellow and greasy, fetid, stinking
Forced out by the flood.

Harley Hill

RAT TAILED WANTING | 040

Long tailed want gnaws hard,
old friend, grinds at the heart,
digests old dreams, defecates
desires we never had when young.
Our days of poverty are gone —
days we walked through Simi heat,
pregnant with hope, dreams packed
tightly, seeping out our eyes. We
have made it, as they say, made
a thousand deals, made a life,
made our bed, and lie here panting.
This rat tailed want gnaws holes,
masticates those younger days.

John Sweet

WEIGHING THE WORD LOVE ON BROKEN SCALES | 041

how many years now wasted
weighing the word *love*
on broken scales?

there is no religion
to be found here
only stigmata
and the taste of dust

empty room
after empty room until
you finally reach the one
you call home

in this corner
a man shot in the face
from less than a
foot away

in that one
the woman who loves pain
screaming for the baby
she never had

you will become
one or you will become

the other and
either way
your future has been
determined

there is nothing left
but to be
nailed to it

Christopher Swan

SUNSHINE STATE | 042

In wood gray comes
soon before falling down.
Inland Florida being no exception,
across the road a gate creaking
"Keep Out" where the rusty sun sets,
and a seven-year-old girl tore her dress
on the barbed wire fence
behind which a dirt road
disappears in a field of burrs
and weeds and nothing
ever happens.
The sun seems distant,
yet it bakes the air
from horizon to horizon;
and the moon,
when it gets close to the land,
turns maroon, turns the land
a kind of sinister shallow pale.
The three of us watch the
bonfires down the road
set by a man my mother
calls a pyromaniac.
And when my father comes home,
with his usual bright humor,
calling this place "The Ranch,"
she reminds him of the fact

that it is a shack. A gray wood shack.
The shack adds fuel to their nasty fights
this being only the latest, sorriest hole
he's dumped his family in
along a string of failed jobs, binges,
increasingly prolonged absences
...until one final sun-seared afternoon
she drags two suitcases
and her three children down
the long, hot, shimmering road
to catch a bus to another life
bought by her father,
leaving behind only
a letter from a woman,
hotly disputed and in pieces,
blown and scattered on the floor...
Turning back to look, I see the shack.
Dead wood; unkindled by the sun.

Christopher Swan

EARLY LIGHT | 043

If all he had was the chance
to fumble darkly toward a better end,
and grope along his unlit stairway,
he'd have gladly accepted the opportunity,
if only for the feeling he was getting somewhere.
But now he must be content to stay,
to measure out the dimensions of his heart;
Because here, a light burns softly,
even through the hooded lens of his eye;
warm, numinous... illuminating
and, sometime, it tells him,
he will make his way into the crowded days;
single out the faces that seek remembering;
the identifying sorrows etched in every face;
record the time and place of their passing,
like an Etruscan painter whose portraits
left the only traces of a long disremembered
people–that their eyes might gaze,
limpid with futile beauty,
into ours.

Christopher Swan

RIVER RUN | **044**

Time's the river rushing on,
swallows tributary lives,
visible until they're gone.

Push against or pull upon
—life's the thing that just arrives—
Time's the river rushing on.

It's the stream where humans spawn,
wriggle through their dwindling lives,
visible until they're gone.

Earth, wind, and fire carry on:
Drink again what life revives.
Time's the river rushing on.

Take a look at everyone,
know there's meaning in their lives
(time's the river rushing on)
visible until they're gone.

Kelley Jean White

WHAT DO YOU EAT WHEN YOU'RE NOT IN LOVE?

stones
river mud
salted straw

still I don't grow
lean

Stacked

I have a deck
and every card
is the Queen
of Hearts. I deal
my own hand
on the bedspread
solitaire
every face up
card is her
and every back
your hair.

Kelley Jean White
BRITTLE | **046**

angels in the mirror
looking at me
angels in the mirror
I can't see

angels smiling at me
with a laugh
angels glitter at me
breaking glass

look at smoke around me
look wordless
disbelieving angels
look so blessed

seek relief my angels
rose to be
angels in my mirror
laugh with me

angels in my mirror
watching me
angels without voices
breaking free

angels in the ashes

suddenly
glitter little angels
sing to me

glitter little angels
almost done
turn it to the wall
oblivion

put away the pieces
let me be
angels fly around me
set them free

angels left the mirror
just for me

Carol Parris Krauss

LUNCH @ LA BELLE | 047

Down to La Belle
for escargot
garlic-butter gravy drippings
down Kelly's chin
The large lady next
to us reeking of
lavender
toilet water
and adorned with a droopy
chapeau
flies buzzin' in a craze around my crepe
exhaust filters in
the city sounds
certainly not a Monet
lunch @ La Belle
the monsieur in the tropical print
and polyester pants
belches not-so-discreetly
excuse moi
or something like that
cheap blush wine
and
tap water in a cobalt blue bottle
re-corked I believe

lunch @ La Belle
Kelly laughs
the sounds and scenery charm
her
amusant
or something like that
Lunch@La Belle

John Sweet

PROVING DALI'S EXISTENCE WITH WORDS AND THE SPACES BETWEEN THEM | 048

not quite silence in the
gentle hum of early afternoon
but maybe something softer than
the screams of crows

something more human than the
room of hanged men

and how many years now since
my last escape?

how many hours wasted staring into
dirty mirrors or
through warped panes of glass?

what i see is that at
some point in the future i will be
asking my son for forgiveness

at some point
i will speak of my own father
for the last time

will spit out his ashes while
faceless men in the towns i've escaped from
beat their wives and girlfriends with
the brutal fists of love

and one half of the truth
is that i never saved anyone
and the other half
is that i never knew anyone who wanted to be saved

i had nothing better to offer than
the holes that had already
been dug

this is history on a personal level

the possibility of failure
through indifference

of love turning to hate
and then hatred to suicide

and if my mother sheds any tears
over the sudden holes that
appear in her life
i make a point of looking away

if desperate acts of violents leave
any visible scars on the
ones left behind
i don't want to know

i have already
made up my mind to run

Bill Wunder

MEMORIAL DAY 2002 | 049

I'd nearly forgotten that room
but lately, things appear
in the narrow, dark space
between door and linoleum:

Fingertips of palm fronds;
fragments of jungle fatigues;
love beads we wore under them.

Acrid, burning wreckage
of a helicopter delivering mail
and Christmas dinners to a hot LZ.

Foul, strange aroma
of mama-san improvising
meals out of fish heads and rice.

Thunderous roar of F-4 Phantoms
climbing in tandem, urgency in their contrails,
distant varumpf of bombs in mountains.

Sing-song complaints
of mothers moved
from ancestral villages,
their children clinging
to them like jungle vines.

Startled starlings erupt
into the safety of an empty sky
at my best friend's funeral.

Rifle reports from the gleaming
honor guard, me on my way to war,
him, on his way to a cold permanence.

His mother's sobs in the frozen air,
my exhaled breath in January sunlight.

Today is memorial day.
There are picnics, parades,
Wal-Mart is having one of their biggest sales,
and the car dealer in town is offering double rebates.

My hand is on the doorknob, and I hesitate,
wondering if whatever lives in this room
is tame enough now, the pain lessened
enough for me to bear.

Janet Buck

THIS OLD CHAIR | 050

We divided your stuff
on the tail of black limos
creeping the ragged streets.
My sister took the pretty towels –
the ones that said:
"Don't touch, I stain;
Don't fold, I tear.
Don't use, I bite."

All that was left was the lump of a chair
that cradled the crumbling straw.
From here, you argued with walls,
with a god you couldn't see
but chose to trust no differently
than ducks fly south
imbued with promises of warmth.
An afghan draped across the back
to cover holes your spine had rubbed.

From here, you flipped like a caught trout
in the moon's gray pail.
Watched as the rainfall bled on fuzzy portraits of glass.
Listened as the furnace chirped
its bird-like morning arias.
From here, you grabbed an apron string
as love would jet from room to room.

Lit your pipe, gushed about her homemade pies.
Marked her lips with syrup spittle,
afterglow of Sunday waffles on the porch.

This old thing Grandma called
a wart on nice, an albatross of tackiness,
a dog to shoot, a rock to lift –
but never moved and dusted
like a precious mink in closets of the very rich.
Dimes between the cushion cracks.
Songs of sweat on beaten arms.
I had to keep this monument.
All your craters, all your perils,
all your Hells had settled here.

Janet Buck

SO THIS HOW AGAPE READS | 051

Eyes wide open for the Fall –
it's a season as well as a fact.
We can't exchange
these tired carrots of our bones
for brand new pencils in a box.
Consider this a thank you note:
I'm grateful you refuse to skip
the parts of life that tell
our eyes a bomb was here.
All our ankles, all our knees are arguing
with Waterloos of daily chores.
I think of times when touching toes
were take-for-granted music bars.

Five days after surgery,
I roll your socks in condoms
over wet erections of your will.
Vacuum while you shower and dress,
squint in case I'm missing dirt.
Bending down to pick up soiled underwear
could snap the fragile paperclip.
Standing is a stale cracker under weight.
Cheese we were becomes a scar.
We talk apart the wars that won –
go home to rest a thicker shield
as bullets build behind our backs.

These front-row seats of death we own
would make us pale applesauce if not
for specks of cinnamon, of being there
as hours grow bruised, become the worm.
As years play tricks, as menus fade
where sweaty glasses parked their rings,
I ponder how lonely the path would be
without your footprints next to mine.
From bookends sliding down a shelf,
we learn to meter what remains
on pages with their binding loose.
So this is how agape reads –
the seed that makes the jam the jam.

Janet Buck

SHARP ICE | **052**

Your hair was the color of pearls,
but I didn't think they were real.
I couldn't admit to the ash
of your skin, its porcelain pose
on saucers of graves.
Two long days beside your bed.
A cradle I pushed but could not rock.
My eyes were grabbing renaissance.
I knew it but I acted blind.

You warned me of death and its salt –
how oceans are garnished with thirst.
You taught me how to rope and rise
a baby grand from dining rooms
of buried ships – and still I
painted ivory keys of fingernails
neon shades of busy lies
with no respect for waning light.
A wish was stepping on my hands.

Too young to abide the wrinkling fruit,
I wasn't prepared for the rind.
"Consider a storm the polish of craft,
expect the ice to be sharp" – you said,
but I sat deaf ten miles away.
I should have been there,
when the clock of your heartbeat stopped –
darning a prayer for the size of the hole,
as lungs collapsed like old cocoons.

Janet Buck
RUG BURN | 053

I'm five again. Dresses with bows
in the back become an impossible reach.
Mother's death is everywhere – especially
in speechlessness, in flour bags
beneath dark olives of Daddy's eyes.
He's earned this shade of painful pitch.
Phrases that corner her name
rub rocks in the gaping sore, create
a kind of carpet burn when
elbows touch by accident.
My sister tries on all her clothes –
ghostly blouses hang below her shaking knees
like circus tents without their pegs.
She throws them on the bedroom floor
in angry heaps of autumn leaves.
Soon enough we'll learn to sweep,
pull the weeds where flowers grew.

Every trinket in the house –
from dishes to porcelain cats,
from quilts to tables set for three –
business cards with edges curled
smeared with the ink of her grave.
Her shiny brown piano seat
has cobwebs in its antique joints.

A maid comes in to clean the keys
that seem to shrink like bars of soap.
Soon we'll plant a fence or two
as if they're trees and have a place.
He'll water them at cocktail hour,
watch the fog as it fixes
the absent to nothingness.
I stay in the gloves of my skin.
afraid to window-crack a tear.
Questioning the cauterized
with crayons and an empty page,
I draw her name in large red streaks
as if its lipstick colored gray.
Wedding photos disappear.
Another woman's furniture arrives in trucks.
I look for a cushion with pins.

Janet Buck

THE WASTELAND WHERE YOUR BODY SLEPT | 054

In the wake of serpentine limos,
saccharine cards, carnation fields
arranged just so, the water
in Simon's pond went black.
Our house grew laughless, tombstone cold –
spiders ran their gamuts of lace.
It was 1959 – computers hadn't been born,
so Daddy deleted our stringless harps
with gin or a beer, something with ice
and a fragrance that stung.
I sensed it was our medicine.
I thought I should learn to pour.

Sunday was our lazy hour –
a game of camping under sheets.
The mattress seemed a vacant lot
some CAT had cleared by accident.
Lip of the cotton always infused
with the liquid of eyes.
Exhausted from spearing
unspearable moods like silver trout.
He sent me out to hunt a bear.
My tiny hands came back
with one of your socks still smelling
of leather in shoes that were gone.

I boxed your pillow with a fist
until the feathers left in air
like blackbirds struck by B-B guns.
Father's bed, a wasteland now
where bridges of touch
seemed useless iron.
With rivers dry, no wonder
the lake of our chatter was low.
At barely four, I ran my digits
over the lumps of crumbling coal.
Found rattling gourds of his arms
reaching for flesh in a grave.

Janet Buck

GRAMMY'S TOOLS | 055

The clothesline, Grammy quipped,
is a tree house string with a can
where women gather to swirl
a rumor in lukewarm tea.
Watch your back! she warned.
The birds have ears.
They'll carry a secret around the block.
They learn to sing from listening.
Grampa grinned from old cocoons
of hammocks on the shaded porch.
Aware she was his brick and tree,
his every grain of reasoning.
Amazed at how tortilla flesh
stood up to welcome mats of graves.
Amazed at how she passed the sun
from fingertip to fingertip
as if it were a flaming torch.

Those full-lipped white magnolia smiles
wove lasting garlands in my hands.
She spoke directly to a rose
as if its infant needed her.
Flowers learned to kneel in moisture,
then revolt again toward light.
Epiphany was just a page
of cotton shirts, blood removed,
sleeves relaxed like bygone ghosts.
Her stomach wiggled when she laughed –
bowls of tested gelatin.
An apron for her negligée...
the teeth of a washboard for silk
and a good book of dreams
to balance a menu of hail.

Patrick Seth Williams
UNDERNEATH | **056**

It happens in the middle of the night
when I am dreaming in pastels,
I'll sit up in bed and shiver in the dark,
sweat trickling down my forehead
in the same sickening way it drips
from a faucet with faulty seal.
I'm nauseous, weak; I stand and pace
in my plaid boxer briefs to the bathroom
where the mirror reflects an image
I paid $5 to see at the last carnival.
My taut skin making my veins
look varicose in the glow of the vanity.
I run to the kitchen screaming:
there are scars underneath my skin
awaiting a knife to uncover them.

Patrick Seth Williams

GINSBERG AT BREAKFAST | **057**

Blueberry pancakes, strawberry syrup
news broadcast of Bush's war
how different the world is for us

And you Allen, did you have correct change
and are sitting on the bank of the river
dangling your feet, calloused
from insomniac narcotic walks through Berkeley
where Whitman stood under street lamps
and in grocery stores tempting you
with the body of a young boy

have you taken off your fedora, or put it on
sing me a bar of Spanish loyalist song
or read me poems
I'm no brother, I'm your son
though I've seen only 20 sides 'America
can I hide among the whiskers of your beard
we can find reindeer to fly us to the moon
and talk to god, which one is not important
I'm waiting, as long as I'm able

Patrick Seth Williams

VOODOO MANIFESTATIONS | **058**

The dead have risen.
They walk the streets
at night, in search
of a promised rapture.

One-by-one they file
into empty jazz clubs,
to pick up instruments,
and play for lost arts.

Some take turns
scatting into the mic
to the sound of bongos
and berry saxophones.

Others recline back
in their chairs, smoke
cigars, and nod along
approvingly.

They aren't voodoo
manifestations, but
flesh and blood human
beings back from

the last great pool hall.
This their only time
to walk among streets
of their dreams, and do

the things they did
while living. They
must return when
the doors open up

for business. Though,
many wish to go out
and crawl up to their
children's windows.

the thought of being
just an apparition
is too much to bare.

Christine Hamm

HYSTERICAL BLINDNESS | 059

My life is pain.
I could be a hypochondriac.
There's some kind of multiple choice here,
but I lost the pencil and forgot to mark the page.

I'm not quite sure – I wake up sick
in the morning, nauseated by all the light.
My feet leaving the mattress
for the floor gives me shooting pains
somewhere.

I'd have to ask my doctor,
but she stopped returning my calls last month.
She said it was getting too intense
between us,
all that blood and exchange of bodily fluids.

She had a thing for latex.
I think that shows a fear of intimacy.
We only kissed twice the whole time
we were together.
Anyway, it's over now.
She won't even renew my prescription
for codeine.

And I'm left with this migraine

and an unnatural swelling behind my left ear.

My skin, it tingles

sometimes, along my fingertips.

I'm sure it's the precursor

to some sort of paralysis.

And the light, ah,

the light!

It scalds my eyes.

Makes them tear constantly.

This can't be normal.

Tell me, this can't be

normal.

John Sweet

AMONG THE DEAD AND DYING | 060

there are rooms
in this house filled with
nothing but the black weight
of your past

there are windows pushed
to the point of breaking

and being in love is
being on the wrong side of
a locked door and i
find myself too often forgetting
where i've left the sun

i find myself
numbered among the dead
and dying species while
further down some long unused hallway
you cry for the person i've
made you become

and we will find each other in
the last fragile seconds
before the sky splits open
and we will stop

our hands will
explore living flesh beneath the
first low mutters of thunder and
our tongues will follow

that we believe this much in
the force of desire
should never be forgotten

Janet Buck

YOLKI BLUES | 061

I am the yolki flower, the shade of an egg.
I arrive in a burst, albumen and sack,
after first treasure of rain.
I promise you things.
Your soil is deaf to my voice,
a signal of centering force.
I am Israel's daffodil, a trumpet the poets
have bellowed through dust.
You are the frost with your habits and hands
holding a gun to temples of peace.

I shimmy with sunlight and birth.
Yet, darkness is all I'm coming to know.
Why are you plodding on trails
of a tomb in the guise and the guess
of slicing an earth meant to be shared.
Insisting on fences and walls kilometers long.
Old battles and shrapnel are eating my leaves.
In other wars, no stones, no wires
were enough to contain a rampage of terror.

A pendulum swings, cracking the clock.
This flavor of hate shrivels my flesh.
Piranhas are grabbing whatever moves.
Our quibbles are ancient sheep
gnawing the throat of an innocent lamb.
It didn't work for Berlin,
where the Dipper shoveled a grave
and Pleiades became a fixture
of glory removed in bullets exchanged –
where shadows grew sharp,
sticky with blood,
in palettes of crippling swastikas.

John Sweet

VAN GOGH TAKES UP PAINTING AGAIN, 122 YEARS AFTER HIS SUICIDE | 062

grey light
edged with purple

the age of dogs returned

the taste of frost
on metal

of rust

the motor grinding against
the sky's blood
and nothing else

no heat
no motion
no gentle music

a language
but not one you recognize

whispers and screams

nothing in between
and your hands numb

the fingers cracked
and bleeding

the taste of gasoline

a simple violence and
you swallow

Janet Buck

ALLERGIES TO IVORY | **063**

I understood your allergies to ivory,
anything close to white. Perhaps it was
a form to sign inside the morgue.
Vivid frost of lonely winters
after cancer shook the house,
left you only furniture
and pitch black night
without much velvet in its grain.
The livid shade of feckless hope,
of failure knocking at the door.
The color was that pat, that clean.
Death is the ultimate bleach.
The parking lot had memories
of times your shoes kicked a tire,
then returned to dust a shelf of china cups
that rattled in an avalanche.

"I'll call you on the phone," you said,
"but I can't walk the ghostly halls."
I understood the jail rails of steel beds
and gurneys that carry a world away –
then lie and do not bring it back.
That room with little on the walls but
voiding charts and memos to a passing nurse
who had no answers in her hand
but gentle ways to close the book

as raison d'être lost its glue.
I would have picked the dye myself.
Every lily told a tale
of love as poisoned manuscripts.
Anything in dirty chalk
was just too close to missing angels,
open graves, and pale moans.

Janet Buck

ASSUMPTION | 064

It's been two years, one month, three weeks,
four days.
Since I sat on the edge of her bed
reading "Dover Beach" aloud
for ears pressed firmly
to the final page of life.
Patches of strength
curling their corners
like bandaids over wetted skin.

And I thought I could.
Make crepes that smiled from the pan
and press her Irish linen
without the steam of tears
and tuck it out of sight.

We matched like new pairs of socks
in my underwear drawer
or widows holding hands at Sunday Mass.
I'm sure she knew I smoked
and never said a word.
But turned faux pas like broken lips
of china cups around to face the wall.
It's been two years, one month, three weeks,
four days.

And I thought I could.
Sit on her bathroom floor alone.
Use wine to take me places I needed to go.
She had this way –
of revising defeat –
of pouring waterfalls of misery
into margarine tubs
and sending me home,
steering straight.

I still feed the daisies she left
with watered gin, and they flower
even in September's shade.
Each book she bound with patient flesh.
Advice a gilded potpourri
sprinked like sugar
over bowls of regret.

We both agreed that bridge
was a waste of precious hours.
That poetry and shoehorns
wedged crippled toes
into the "best of times."
It's been two years, one month, three weeks,
four days.

And I thought I could.

Keith Webb

SO MUCH LESS THAN SENSUAL | **065**

this is a picture
or more of
a window into a
roadside bar, where
trucks parked on gravel
surround
a place I know
too well to be tranquil,
a place for solemn meditation,
mediation between my things.

although subtle thoughts get
broken apart by the occasional
loud mouth stepping up,
what he sees as his life's work,
is a seldom at bat,
and there is peace here
more often than at home alone.

inquiring for a menu with my beer,
the cute as a baby-doll girl that came
for my order
wondered later why I had barely
touched my steak sandwich,
a patty, unfrozen and
fried in a skillet, so much

less than sensual, laid out equally
such a waste of a cow's life,
and I say, "It's okay.
I didn't come here to eat."
she replies, "I understand."
but then how could she
know of so many things
waitress
barkeep
Nostrodamus.

M. R. Benning

CURLED AND JARRED | **066**

as if something sparked a memory
of birth at two-forty-seven
on a Sunday
during a rainstorm.

Inside his narrow cot,
an itchy issued blanket —
coarse as the accented words and
foreign fingers wrapped around
his conditioned thigh.

"Vat yoo doo to me izt art,"
is exhaled as
breasts are flattened
against his back and
hair to his lips
like leaves to
moist concrete.

M. R. Benning

THE BIOLOGY OF JIMMY SMITH | 067

The skin of his hands is cracking
as Jimmy Smith becomes
subject to his first
in-class erection.

It is because of Mrs. Dopleworth,
the blue flower dressed
middle school teacher
preparing simple science notes
on a tall screeching blackboard.

She scrawls:
Some facts about your toads,

and the dress rises,
agitating little Jimmy in his
wiggling plastic bucket seat.

"The eardrum is located here.
It's also known as the
tym-pan-ic mem-brane."

Her floral short sleeve
flushes out a bit
while she syllabically points,
opening to a
black bra strap.

Watching without listening,
his feet crinkle
like foil on the
linoleum floor.

Staring at Jimmy:
"You're allowed to touch
your toad."
leaves her lips while
she brushes
baby powder chalk against those
midnight blue petals.

Jimmy aches to see them
wilt from her body
and collapse on the floor.
The same way he would,
if she whispered that
statement into his skinny ear.

He thinks of her lips so close
and rubs his hands together,
brushing off
tiny wistful flakes of himself
in a jarring
heart thumping moment.

Janet Buck

INSIDE A NAME | 068

I whisper her name aloud –
you tug at a chair to gather your coat,
pet the dog and say goodbye
before a question
kicks you in the tender groin.
Your eyelids curtsy once and clench –
a mirror of the coffin's hinge.
I'd like to follow roads you take,
through briars of the fruitless vines,
down sharp, dry cliffs
that crumble at the slightest wind.
Our silence is my orphanage,
but you don't know the windows
you have blocked from light.

Hand me just a sweater's sleeve,
some syntax, context, anything
that spells the way she made the bed
into a novel packed with lust
and happiness now cherry pits.
Her memory is snow in summer,
smelly oil on concrete floors
of some garage I sense is cold.
Nearly fifty years have passed.
Sores should own a scar or two,
but closure is impossible
without exposure to the air.

I'd like to follow roads you take,
even if this island has no sustenance
and storms direct the weather vanes.
Death might have been a melody
we rode until the song came back.
I step on leaves around her grave,
hear the crunch of missing heels,
stay the hungry hummingbird,
who cannot find the center
of a rose removed –
wings on fire for searching
through the muted spring.

Janet Buck

SUDDENLY IT'S SOLITAIRE | 069

One moment he's pruning a wayward branch;
garden tools rest happily against
the brick like spoons in soup.
You wonder how it stayed this warm.
An ancient sun is baking leaves, raisins
in a rising dough of seasons on a schedule.
He edges grass the way he's always
sculpted love – by doing things
in steady gestures like the rain.
A seizure, then a surgery.
Then solitaire so suddenly.
Feet aren't there to track rich soil;
welcome mats have lost all words.

I bake two pies and take
two pieces down the street.
It's a short walk and a long hill
up to the crown of thorns.
The first thick snow is blowing
blizzards of his death as if
some crazy heaven dropped a sack of flour
and all the meals I'm handing you
are just reminders of the cold.
I ring the bell, its tired fly
catches in the vivid freeze.

A single placemat at the bar
stares back at us as if
no cards but this exist.
Boots are empty lecture notes
reminding me that luck
is amputated by the hour.
His coat is hanging like a ghost
beside a hat that buckles
in our winded sighs.
A living room of Roman girth –
spotless but for photographs
you finger in the night's abyss.

John Sweet

PHOTOGRAPHING THE CIVIL WAR | 070

not shadow but
reflection

february rain from
tanguy's sky until the streets
are all dull grey mirrors

if i keep my distance
i could be anyone

if i get in my car and drive
i could call it escape

could call it running away
which is sometimes an act of
cowardice and sometimes
an act of survival

and i sit in this room of
empty chairs instead
with my thoughts
and my bitter resentments

i believe in gorky at the age of 43

in rothko at the age of 66
but not in my father

not at any age and not in any
of the bars i spent my childhood in

i remember the threats
and all of the dire predictions

i remember fifteen years
spent perfecting the
art of silence

what a sad fucking
victory it's become

Janet Buck

A SPEECH BEFORE THE SPLATTERED BLOOD

The DOW spikes up, banking on
a dwarfish draft of Armageddon gloom.
Our president will speak at five.
No casualty is casual.
It's hard to match a suit and tie
to splatter of the coming blood.
Ahmed, a driver in Iraq, says:
"This is a miserable life.
We spent it shopping for war
or hiding from bombs."
He recites his summary
as if his time is finished as a boiled egg.
All eyes red from pressing
night's extended weight.

Justice spelled so many ways our alphabets
no longer know their proper forms.
Iraqis seal their windows shut as if a roll
of tape will come between the fragile glass
and force of missiles jetting
through the tainted sky.
Stirring the hostile soup.
It seems the only spoon we own,
yet who can watch the broth of freedom
dwindle to a water drop.
Have you ever sat on a fence,

answerless and trembling,
wishing posts were firm mirage?

I swing like heavy pendulums
between the prayer to end this horror
and nightmares of approaching graves.
The writer with no salving words,
no sonnets in a pocketbook.
No talons on the olive branch,
no wings of doves, no angels near
as embassies evacuate, as guns replace
the meetings of our shattered hearts
now beetles under heavy boots.
Philanthropy or wet revenge –
I can't decide and so I kneel
as quicksand travels to my chin.

Robert Bohm

MOUNTAINS | 072

A perimeter the mind can't cross,
there they are, barren and austere.
Only the heat outwits them, its haze, a flock
of gray birds, lifting them
back a little further so there's more room for us to go
in and out of the casinos.
Through an alley door, into
a sultry song's midday dark.
As Rachel sings, I listen from backstage.
The last time I saw her: ten years ago when
as now
no known highway connected keyboards and bass
or the scatted sounds that brought
clinking ice cubes to a halt; even
the jazz haters were afraid to make a noise.
It doesn't really matter if I understand
she sings
It doesn't really matter if he's still my man.
It doesn't matter until she makes it matter, her cheekbones
in the piano-taunted light
petroglyphs carved in red sandstone east
of the Moapa River, telling us
how the long-gone soon becomes the just-appeared.
At the ends of streets, mountains
disappear where ex-ranchers
with gnarled hands

play blackjack on sidewalk tables.
Among them, Isaiah, home at last, sips tequila and gazes
at the desert, remembering how
years ago he walked out there
with God as all around them
stones burst into flame. Days later
smoke still rose from the blackened land
as the hawk screamed and the jackal, waking
in God's lap, announced
"My child Isaiah has shown the world
things that he himself doesn't understand."

Robert Bohm

SACRED | 073

The chicken's claw leaves
a mark in dirt, a sign
of questions to be answered.

This
at the city's edge
where the sunflower
snagged on a barbed wire fence
bleeds.

The stranger looks around.
His young daughter's
hands shake.
In the grass
near a telephone pole
the dying butterfly's wingbeats slow.

In a syringe
of denial, the holy water boils
not far from where a man mows a lawn
while a woman on a porch
drinks something from a glass.

Sunset long gone
your shoulder darkens somewhere else in the dusk.

Tomorrow in church
the priest will scar our faces
with light squeezed from the lizard's eyes.

He will say,
"Repeat after me:
Now we are sacred.
Now we can love."

Barclay Kenyon

FIREGARDEN (TRIPTYCH 3)

I. Child
Child
Flesh trophy
For so many nights, I breathed out your name
I breathed out life, and you flew out on the slide…

Now you're here
like an oxcart is here — plumped with harvest
and, before you focus, I wrap
the smoky cloak around me.
We go forth, planting crucifixes in the neighborhood, you and I –
we trade stares. Your eyes immense and bold
and your skin a miracle of profit and galvanism
but the measures of doubt you foment in me,
oh, I take them like cake
and lick the umbilicus for the blessings…

Build you up — I am the waterwheel
Bearer of casks and night tidings
The flowering you've brought to this Garden is my every hope
and convinces me of the secret you'll be hiding

Dress you down — I am the cannibal
Performer of ritual and drag dressings
I'll paint you proud of the bloodsong in your veins
but the melody will have you confessing

Now, listen close, my little spawn
to all that I may say
before I package,
lick you thin
and mail you away

II. A Dead Map
There is the map
There is the tower where my fraudulent claims were called on
to be rent apart by kings and their sycophants and then
thrust out the open windows

I know very little beyond that,
beyond the dead map

There is the name that is always on the tip of my tongue
that pounds through the waves at high tides
and sings through the suns

There is the silhouette of a woman upon a cross
with her legs exquisitely matched and
my heart in a kindergarten chair
beneath her

I know very little beyond that,
those nails and those suns

There is a crying out in the backwater tombs in
the middle of the night, from the whippoorwill haunts —
a craven, bewildered shrieking that strikes V's of birdflight
from the treelines out into the skies

I know the sound of my little boy dying
for his voice is like mine

...but I know very little beyond that

III. The Cycle Begins
The cycle begins with the red seeds of warfare
the apostles and their blankets wet with dew
in the Garden where he made his peace
and they made him stew

The cycle begins
with the aspect of wasps taut with no-mind eyes
running with dust up the chimneys in the boroughs
where the maids ladle cream and
rub salt into their thighs

The cycle begins
with the essence of sanctuary bought by a traveler for a song
it costs ten years of hard labor to you or I and our delusions
but for a swallow-hearted Orpheus and his three-dollar bills
it doesn't take that long

The cycle begins with the unfolding of the ocean
each day of our love with the dawn
comes a hurricane to empty it of baleen and our briny transfixions
then we'll passover to you
what cards we've been drawn

Arlene Ang

THEY SAY | **075**

Good poetry is coming
to the point quickly is not
allowing your reader
time to think is making monkey
out of senses is sky with
pepper ducks is stench
of scorpion beetles rocking
on their backs is warthog
singing the blues is mother's
cooking going well
for once is your reader
suddenly slapping forehead
with hand and saying
damn that is exactly how I feel.

Arlene Ang

FINAL DRAW | 076

For forty-eight years my father
matched his luck with SuperEnalotto.
Tuesdays and Fridays he prepared
after-dinner numbers.
His eyes would close in concentration
to receive divine help
behind steepled hands.
One day, he loved to say,
I'll make my bed on Italian liras.
What he wouldn't say was he hated
minding cars in a gas station
instead of criminals in a courtroom.

Even now cathetered to
a hospital bed, he pleaded me
to play his numbers for him.
You'll see, he whispered
as if I was his alibi in murder,
this time I'm going to win,
then you can go back to college.
I turned away in sudden pain.
That was something I'd never do
even for a million gold bars.

Next day I played his card
and waited for the evening draw.
Afterwards I thanked God
that the room he shared with
six mutating patients
was spared of television,
that hospitals close early to visitors.
Next morning one of the nurses
confessed over the phone
that my father had succumbed to sleep.
With caught regret, I feared
he already knew how Saturday night ended.

Duane Locke

SOLITUDE OR ISOLATION | 077

Learnt late the truth,
Late was alone
As alone as when
With another
In a dark balcony
Or at a dark dinner,
Candle lit and dim.
Mendacity, the mother virginal,
Mastered the poppies and my life.
At the fine feasts,
Mendacity the host, the servant,
The friend, the lover,
Deserter, betrayer.
At these ballistic banquets
There was not as in Veronese,
A small, spotted dog on paws
Under the tablecloth
To sniff and eat the crumbs.
The cardiac malfunction
Of the reticent, false fable
That is transported in skeleton form
By serrations of the unknown superpower
From frowns and smiles
As the face leaps over the hurtles of love and hate.
The fable fastened on the wedding ring finger,
A promise of a thumb rubbing across a knuckle,

Or the concealed pressing together of ankles.
But the world became a dandelion's fuzzy, silk seed,
Whirled from no time of designations to a sunrise bud
That unfolded new hours,
Whose undesigned destinations spattered the precedents.
Now the absent dog wags his unseen tail,
And barks friendly.
I have become secure in isolation,
No longer battle the truth.

Duane Locke

LET ME BE SO | **078**

Let me be so, there are no circles,
Only imperfect chalk and ink sketches
Only awkward imitation on silk,
Algorithmed by allegorists
Who have never been in the bat's cave
Or been shaped by shadows from the overhead bird
That blocks out the illusory light and five-pointed stars.
Let me be so, what was thought to be infallible,
The cadence of corkscrew, blonde curls,
Is now an anachronism, a coffee table conversation piece,
A midriff out of date, replaced by the gospel of cognac.
Let me be so, alone, let me never hear common words.

Rebecca Jung

POEM BEFORE A WAR | 079

On the cusp of a war,
it makes perfect sense
to write of the warm weight
of your body cradling mine, the way
you grip me where thigh meets torso
pulling me into your thrusts,
your fingers pressed deep in my pale flesh,
how you pin me to the bed
your damp chest on my breasts,
the feeding frenzy of our mouths
tasting each other's blood-flushed bodies.
Limb on limb, arms akimbo,
gristle on bone and shit-stained gore,
the curve of a head in the crook of some arm,
the pulsing feast of maggots
on the blackened bodies of Verdun, at Auschwitz,
and the mass graves of Sarajevo—
and a poem
of your singularly precious body
on mine.

Rebecca Jung

THE COLLARBONE | **080**

What is it with me, this obsession? Is it
a simple matter of attraction?
If it were, it could have been
any number of people. There are
other men here who have—can you believe it?
shown an interest in me.
Intelligent, attractive men.

No, it's not that, and gee
but does he realize this, much less care?
He caught me once staring at the little bit
of throat and chest he'd bared
when he unbuttoned his white dress shirt.
I was caught like a man who talks to you
without once looking at your face.

So now, he wears his shirts unbuttoned
past his collarbone when we work together
smiling, watching me
all the while. Jesus.
Just to press my lips to his collarbone.
Never before have I endured
such casual cruelty.

Janet Buck

THE POOLSIDE CHAT | 081

Three women lounge beside a pool –
comparing scars and silently,
the sizes of a spreading waist.
Laughing at the family branches,
reading stories for reprieve.
Different brands of syllables
to suit the weight of sorrow's cloth
and longing, well, it hangs
in sacks beneath the eyes
behind their shades –
it hangs in every swaying elm.

Children cackle in the water,
race across the hot cement
to blankets of their mothers' arms.
Dancing like a moonbeam's stripe
toward that grand chameleon, death,
unaware that bodies
are tenuous treasures at best.
Denominators of the years
will water sadness tacitly.
The chairs are facing east
where light arrives and doesn't stay.

One discusses discipline
for nine year olds

who think a mouth is meant
to tell their father off.
Another, brands of tanning cream
that fake a blush for summer months.
The third is reading Lucy Grealy,
hiding titles under towels
that also drape a half a leg.
She's the one who wears her grief
like stains across a white lapel.
She's the one reminding them
that shaving pairs of flawless thighs
is running digits through dazzling silk.

Kelley Jean White

BRICKHOUSE BLUES | 082

Brickhouse Blues

See these men out shooting craps
up against the brickhouse wall,
these men all shooting craps
up against that brickhouse wall,
hear them dice click on the pavement,
see them dollars fall.

Here come this little man
bouncing his basketball,
along come a little man,
bouncing a basketball,
hair all done up in plaits,
don't hear his Mama call.

See him fanning out his hand,
see eleven—twelve dollar bill,
he be fanning out his hand,
got eleven—twelve dollar bill,
lays 'em on the sidewalk
and that grifter start to shill.

If I had me a dime
I wouldn't play you wicked game,
no, not even a dime,

I wouldn't play that wicked game,
I'd hold up my head,
walk right by you all the same.

Woman walk by
she got two big mean-eyed dogs,
woman walking by,
with those two big mean-eyed dogs,
they go snarling at those mens,
all those useless little dogs.

Joseph Armstead

ANGEL AMONGST ASHES | 083

The sign on the hill
Has the marks of muddy
Boot treads on it and
It is sinking in the mud and ash.

Ageless eyes
that beheld the wonders
Of the endless spaceways
and
The glories of the cosmos
Blink back cold tears.

He is alone.
The wind fans his hair
And it smells of old fires,
Storms,
Wet concrete and rusted steel.
He listens for the silence.

His wounds bleed.
Here there once were kings,
in this place of shattered brick,
rubble,
and they held sway over nations
and armies of fearsome might.

He sees Time
Pass like the waters of
An infinite river, no stone
Touched
By the same water twice,
As the embattled world decays.

He is forever,
All that exists around him is not.
All that burns, smouldering, will fade,
Crumbling
Into dim memory for descendents
Of proud warriors and greedy lords.

Curtains of blood
Descend on the last dark act of
A passion play with no audience,
Applauding
The ghosts of war-torn history
And the sad last pages of the future.

Immortal eyes,
Like twin stars,
See the sign that lies in the
Wet ashen muck, and read
The words

"You Can Save"
and the tears that fall
thereafter are hot and bitter.

The sign on the hill
Is covered by gray ash and
Obsidian smoke as the
Mud swallows it whole.

Janet Buck

MUSTARD SEEDS | 084

I question the empty page
like a moldy slice of bread –
it might have been a decent meal
in someone else's hands.
The clock records a passing hour.
Still no verse worth printing out.
A filthy kitchen floor
sticks to my shoes like an uttered lie –
I flip through yesterday's mail,
stacking bills in heavy bricks,
thinking I'm an ad for grief,
ought to get different life
that dwells upon a butterfly.

Our puppy slams the keyboard tray,
pulls at my socks with rollicking teeth.
Her tail wags east then west –
pointing out with clarity the aching light
I'm missing in this clouded room –
all the blinds pressed
firmly shut like coffin lids.
She rolls upon her fluffy back,
offers me her tender skin
and clammy paws fresh from
morning's dewy lace –
she knows somehow that suns
aren't jars of mustard seeds
to stash on racks and never use.

Rhonda Ward

MISSING LIMBS | **085**

Mostly she misses
his left leg
shorter than the right
the bend in his right knee
when his left leg fell into step
the thirty-degree angle
the wrinkle in the leg of his pants
the perfect point of the crease
as he stepped into his
right-legged stride
the rise and fall
the space between
the space
the leg
the war
the life
the loss

Rhonda Ward

BETWEEN SCHOOL AND HOME | **086**

School is behind me, home before, and between,
this blue-black face with red-pink lips
and weekend breath catcalls from across the street.

His hat-wearing swagger balances on the breeze,
outstretched arms, bent knees. Bloody eye whites
drink me in as if I were the brown-bagged bottle
he wears in his pocket with lint and loose change.

He does not need to say what he wants. I am nine
and already a woman (that's what my mama told me
the day I woke up—cut', screaming for an ambulance).

I am all bright-eyed, new-woman fear;
and the Samaritan arrives only after my socks
have fallen under the explosion of my bladder.

I walk quickly the rest of the way. Home,
I hole up in my room, say nothing to no one.
But nights I dream, scream, wake, remember.

Rhonda Ward

PORTRAIT OF THE PORCH IN SUMMER | 087

There are faded lines where he erased, then stretched,
the too-short porch, made the windows larger,
straightened the steps to the multi-paned door
on the two-dimensional replication of the latchkey
house where he returned sometime after three,

weekdays. The curtains are closed and still
behind shut windows. No breeze to blow
ghost sheers aside to sneak ripple glances
of the empty jar of promises he opened
each day to deposit jail-cell covenants
fragile as Dead Sea scrolls.

He draws a precise facsimile,
crayon memories of ten-year-old summers
sitting on the steps of the porch
chin shoved into the seat of his palm,
awaiting his father's release.

Rhonda Ward

GRAY MATTER | **088**

Her hairline sits back from her face
Like moonlit fields of wheat far from a dusty road.
Wispy strands of gray.

Her brain is mixed, pulled,
twisted circus taffy. Her thoughts
transgress to how her husband

left without a word. She gave
her best to diapers and dinners.
There are only empty plates

and pans. In a bowl she mixes
colors—covers the gray.

Janet Buck

A ROSE TO PRESS | 089

Illness smells out the trite like beagles
with noses near to the ground –
like a mother who knows
her daughter's been smoking
in the bathroom downstairs
a dozen walls away from her.
Suddenly this narrowing
of breakdown lanes, of space to roam,
sidewalks cracking from the ice.
Slippery sunsets, stretching winters,
each hour of spring fresh popcorn
to a starving duck.

Truth becomes too short to hold –
like mustache trimmings in the sink,
like bones that go brittle and snap,
like hay that meets immutable rain.
Don't we wish it didn't take
a teapot growing cold and chipped
to make us want the chamomile.
The poem is a rose to press;
the rose is a poem to read –
this might be it
for both the garden and the light.

c. e. laine

WHY I WROTE MY FIRST LIVING WILL | 090

it was not the way a tube was jammed
into her throat like a drinking straw
shoved through the plastic lid of a frozen malt

it was not the last remark
she scribbled onto the message board
because words were unavailable

it was how her hands were tied
to the stainless-steel bed rails
after they took away her black marker

John Sweet

A SMALL DOG, BLEEDING | 091

it happens this way sometimes,
where the children die from the poison that
seeps up from underground

you vote for one person or the other,
and the children die, and it's not war but
business, and both words are actually just
different ways of saying *profit*

listen

new computers will be given to
the schools as gifts

the sharpened teeth of priests will snap
the bones of young boys in two

what you need to believe in are
rabid dogs
speaking w/ the voices of humans

what we do is use the word *political*
to describe what we don't want to
talk about and then, of course,
the children die

the war becomes nothing more than
one more mundane fact of life,
and the men who make money off of
the corpses of every dead soldier,
and that there are others out there
filming your daughters fucking faceless strangers

that the poem is just a message
handed down from the
throne of god

you will ignore it like all of
the lies you've been forced to swallow
in the past, and then it will come
to define you

John Sweet

FIRST PORTRAIT OF MARIA, IN THE STYLE OF DALI

You in this sepia-toned photograph,
with your arms wide open in greeting,
with your hands held up in surrender.

Edge of highway, corner of house,
hint of something better. A body of water,
maybe, or the back of someone else's
head.

A gun pulled from inside the
killer's heart, and he says *Mr. Lennon*,
then smiles, then pulls the trigger.

No.

I've gotten ahead of myself here.

I'm ten years old and in a boat with
my father and two of his friends, and the
engine has died. The tide is going out,
and the only sound is the pull of the
ocean.

The only heat is the
mindless glare of the sun.

I don't know you yet,
haven't fallen in love with you,
haven't let my tongue flicker lightly
across your nipples in a
curtained room.

The story is over,
or is possibly just beginning.

I have the picture, but can never
make out the expression on your face.

Michael Lee Johnson
DOVE POEM | 093

I hear
scratch of
little dove feet.
I hear peck
of little dove bills
in bird seed basket
on my balcony—
in near silence
on rain-filled
afternoon—
lightning,
thunderstorm
overhead darkness,
cramped up with rage,
holds off a minute
so I may
hear these sounds.

Erik Austin Deerly
KENT | **094**

I love you, I told him
Meals on wheels didn't come 'til three o'clock
He's pissed
I love you too, he said, trying to swallow it back down
*
Rewind, thirty years:
Leisure suit and perm aside,
Dad's never changed
Trouble with women, he says, *they just want to be happy*

He never remarried
Thanksgiving with my Mom—Christmas with Dad
I came home after college
He was an old man
*
He reads glossy magazines
Schools me on pop culture
On his 78th birthday he asked for *Moby*
Though lately he prefers punk

When I was young, I had this dream my dad was shot
in the chest with a cannonball
He came home in this dream; I could see right through
the big round hole
The wound was clean, as if he were made of cookie dough
I couldn't bring myself to touch him

*

Gave my dad a hug the other day
We repaired his iTunes
Picked over cold lunchmeat
Snapped a few pictures, said goodbye

Three days later—snail-mail from Dad
Scrawled across the back of a carefully folded article
About Balinese Hip-Hop:
I love you, too

Erik Austin Deerly

DEAR HARVEY | 095

I went to your memorial last Thursday
but you were not there
in your place was an old photo
you on your horse
full head of poorly cut hair
accidentally hip.

The woman spoke about energy, afterlife
and rejoining your ancestors.
While we bowed our heads
you reached into your holster
drew your revolver
and took pot shots.

If you didn't want your bronzed baby booties displayed in public
you should've mentioned it while you had the chance, cowboy.

Madeleine J. Deerly (1938-2009)

**SOME THINGS I HAVE LEARNED THAT
I WOULD BE MUCH BETTER OFF NOT KNOWING**

well here I was, facing another locked drawer without a key,
and not just metaphorically, although there is that.
thinking more crap that you accumulated and left me to deal with;
more coins, more stamps, more bills, a neatly
rubber-banded bundle of Publishers Sweepstakes entries
never sent in but saved because god knows why.
all that junk in my basement. a car that no one wants,
cowering in dusty mortification and leaking oil
all over a dozen or so cartons
containing nothing useful as far as I can see.
and I think, oh what a lovable idiot you were, you great big doofus
what a warm and funny simple guy, and wasn't I lucky
to be the one you loved and left all this mess?
and wasn't life more interesting and full because you were so careless
about the details, like putting the car title where someone could find it?
and wasn't I just telling someone the other day
about how none of this mattered because you and I were always
so crazy about each other?
and isn't it ironic now that I have to pay some guy $65
to drill out this lock and find this little pile of what will turn out to be
love letters from the Polish lady who took care of your mother?
yes, the very one for whom I wrote the glowing reference,
although my intention was not to refer her to you.
to whom was I talking, when I thought I was talking to you?
and just how long did you think it would take
for me to turn this into material?

JE Baker

TRAIL | 097

The doe is dead, devoured by hounds.
Her bones lie by the river's edge.
Curled small,
small is never long;
her body will grow and cast away the brush that veils her.
Her fair spots will fade with time.
It's the sparrows that call her to run,
to stretch her legs long and flee.
But the fawn, she listens to the leaves
whispering that it is safe to stay.

I stood at the sink
scratching and scraping until fingertips were bloodied and sore.
As the water ran I thought,
her spine curved like the back of my ear —
her heart in a box.

It's easy for the leaves to die.
The mantle of dirt shows the way.
Head south,
toward the river;
blood smothers the earth where half-eaten bones are still strewn.
Ash-covered tracks form a trail.
The Huntsman keeps her heart in a box,
to take to his aging Queen.
But from there an iris still watches,
warning her daughter never to stay.

The water was hot
and the steam held a stench like a scream at the back of the throat.
My eyes burned, but I knew
she hadn't had time to not be timid —
she breaks like the doe.

Hidden, hooves tucked up underneath.
She rises and stamps on the ground.
Look at them,
her feet ashen;
slight and unsteady as they search for a suitable trail.
She won't fall to the arrow.
The Huntsman thinks she breaks like the doe,
running, her tail in the air.
But the white flag isn't surrender,
waning fear frees her heart lest she stay.

Ivor Irwin

MARRIAGE | 098

I explain. You
hear shouting. You
regroup. I see
you've picked my scab.
You are reasonable. I
see shades clipped onto your bifocals. I
apologize profusely. You
sniff out expedience.
I am a nice Jewish dove. You
say I'm crazy, like Saul. You
throw me an olive branch. I
am cut by its thorns.
You gush blood. I
see no tears. You
will not take a dive. I
have loved you for eleven years.

Ivor Irwin

6 A.M.- 9 A.M. | 099

The snow may be 9½" deep, but
I'm a resourceful He-Manly man, man.
Up at 5 a.m.
Layering layers upon layers.
I stagger around, puffy, prepared.
Stagger and sass, sass some more,
dawn dreaming in the inky dark.
As the sun slowly rises, grunting
like some 47-year-old ex-NFL quarterback,
I am the magnificent soloist maestro,
wielding my shovel heroically,
I dig a moat around my mansion,
clear the way for my wife and her wee dark-green Honda.
Staggering back inside, I take off some of my layers,
wake the kid, kiss the wife goodbye,
bulk up our bellies with oatmeal,
dress him in layers, vaseline his tiny gob and cheeks.
I relayer myself, and then we go for the bus.
Two grand staggerers on an epic intrepid Dr. Zhivago walk,
bobbing and weaving through dirty gray snowbanks,
which have fresh crunchy snow layering their tops, and,
really, I wouldn't mention the frozen dog shit,
except it's fucking everywhere,
so that 31st is a toxic knickerbocker glory.
When the bus arrives, its engine stuttering as it vibrates against snow banks

I climb up the dirty mountain, lift the boy up and over
and nod at my fellow warrior, the bus driver.
Once home, I peel off my layers. Blow
my nose so hard it hurts my ears,
savor a cup of tea, listen
as my knee cartilage creaks. Listen

as my neighbors struggle to start their engines. Listen
to the ranting on Sports Radio. Wonder
at the warm wire I feel through the muscle in my heart.
Struggling up the stairs, turning up the heat, I
run a bath, spit out snot and get naked.
I bathe, ponder my aging balls.
Look at the clock: 9 a.m.
Now it's under the covers and
sleep.

Notes On The Contributors

Arlene Ang lives in Venice, Italy, as a freelance translator and web designer. She also edits the Italian Niederngasse. Her poetry has appeared in *Poet's Canvas, Scrivener's Pen, Eclectica,* and many others.

Joseph Armstead is a suspense-thriller author, poet and computer technologist. He has authored nine novels, over two dozen short stories and has been published in a dozen magazines and online journals.

JE Baker is a book and paper artist and a writer.

M. R. Benning's brain leaks perversion. It is not intentional. He is simply Freudian and it hurts. How he has taken it upon himself to manifest what you wish you could tell when you were twelve. He is almost there, creeping into everyone and tugging at their memories.

Robert Bohm was born in Queens, NY. He is a poet.

Janet Buck is a seven-time Pushcart Nominee. Her poetry has appeared in *2River View, Offcourse, The Pedestal Magazine,* and hundreds of journals worldwide. Janet's second print collection of poetry, *Tickets to a Closing Play,* was the winner of the 2002 Gival Press Poetry Award. Her third collection, *Beckoned By The Reckoning,* was released by PoetWorks Press in the spring of 2004. Buck teaches writing courses for Rogue Community College and lives in Medford, Oregon.

Michael Carano was featured in issue 11 of *Burningword*.

Christina Croft has published both short stories and poetry. Her writing can be found in *The Murder Hole, Shadowkeep Zine, Dark Moon Rising,* and *Insolent Rudder*.

Erik Austin Deerly is a media artist, designer and composer. He writes poetry, serves as Publishing Editor of *Burningword Literary Journal*, and is cofounder of Burrdowning Press.

Madeleine J. Deerly (1938-2009) was a life-long writer and avid reader of prose and poetry.

Anita Garza is a book and paper artist and has published both short stories and poetry. She serves as Editor in Chief of *Burningword Literary Journal* and cofounder of Burrdowning Press.

Michael William Giberson is a retired criminalist and writer.

Christine Hamm has an MFA in creative writing and has been published in *Shampoo Poetry, Poetry Midwest, Stirring*, and many others.

Harley Hill is a lawyer and writer living on the California Central Coast. She resides, with her dog Roma, in a quaint cottage near an avocado orchard, an orange tree, and a Camellia tree.

Ivor Irwin is a native of Manchester, England. He is the author of *A Peacock or A Crow* and has published writing in *Sonora Review, The Sun, Playboy, Shankpainter, The Long Story, Actos de Inconsciencia, The Review of Contemporary Fiction* and various other journals. He writes a weekly column on Premier League soccer for *Global Football Today*.

Michael Lee Johnson is from Itasca, Illinois. He lived in Canada for 10 years during the Vietnam era and is published in 25 countries. He runs five poetry sites, and published works are available at poetryman.mysite.com, lulu.com, Amazon.com, Barnes & Noble, and iUniverse.

Richard Jordan is a PhD mathematician and a poet. He currently resides in Virginia, where by day, he works on the mathematical modeling and analysis of the spread of infectious diseases, and by night, he tries his best not to contract any such diseases.

Rebecca Jung has been published in *The Pennsylvania Review, Impetus, The Pittsburgh Quarterly, Wazee Journal, MiPo, The Pittsburgh Post-Gazette, CC&D, The Festival of Women's Voices Anthology* and a chapbook titled *The Relic Maker*.

Barclay Kenyon is a psychiatric worker and poet who lives by the water.

Carol Parris Krauss is a poet and teacher. Her poems are quite visual, complexly simple, and usually about the South.

c. e. laine's "why I wrote my first living will" originally appeared in *Stirring*, written under the name Kit Sullivan.

Duane Locke lives in Tampa, Florida, and has had 4,766 poems published. in print magazines and e-zines.

Chad Rood was featured in issue 6 of *Burningword*.

Christopher Swan is a journalist and poet. His work has appeared in *The Boston Globe, The Los Angeles Times*, and in numerous magazines.

John Sweet, born 1968, is married, father of two, and opposed to all that is evil. He has been living in the vast wasteland that is upstate New York for the majority of his life; is a firm believer in writing as catharsis, and in the idea that true democracy is a myth. A full length collection of his work, *Human Cathedrals*, is available from Ravenna Press.

Doug Tanoury is exclusively a poet on the internet, with the vast majority of his work being published online and never leaving electronic form. His verse can be read at electronic magazines and journals across the world.

Sam Vaknin is the author of *Malignant Self Love - Narcissism Revisited* and *After the Rain - How the West Lost the East*. He is a columnist for Central Europe Review, United Press International (UPI).

Rhonda Ward's poetry explores African-American culture with a universal voice, taking everyday situations to visual levels that transport listeners into the world of her childhood with surgical attention to details.

Yun Wei was a high school senior at the time her poems were first published. Her awards already included the 1999 Ray Bradbury Short Story Contest and the Harper College Poetry Contest.

Bill Wunder's poems have twice been nominated for The Pushcart Prize, and in 2004 he was named Poet Laureate of Bucks County, Pennsylvania. His poems have been a finalist in The Robert Fraser Poetry Competition, The Mad Poet's Society Competition twice, and The Allen Ginsberg Poetry Awards three times.

Patrick Seth Williams has degrees in Creative Writing, Nineteenth Century American Literature and Law and Literature.

Kelley Jean White has degrees from Dartmouth College and Harvard Medical School. Her work appears in many poetry journals; her works include a full-length collection of poems related to her medical practice, *The Patient Presents* (The People's Press); a chapbook, *I Am Going to Walk Toward the Sanctuary* (Via Dolorosa Press), and other publications.

Keith Webb is a graduate of West Virginia University with degrees in Journalism, Public Relations, and Creative Writing with emphasis on poetry and short story.

www.ingramcontent.com/pod-product-compliance
Lightning Source LLC
Chambersburg PA
CBHW020803160426
43192CB00006B/423